Jacques Pépin

A Little Golden Book® Biography

By Candice Ransom
Illustrated by Tatsiana Burgaud

Text copyright © 2024 by Candice Ransom
Cover art and interior illustrations copyright © 2024 by Tatsiana Burgaud
All rights reserved. Published in the United States by Golden Books, an imprint of Random House Children's Books, a division of Penguin Random House LLC, 1745 Broadway, New York, NY 10019. Golden Books, A Golden Book, A Little Golden Book, the G colophon, and the distinctive gold spine are registered trademarks of Penguin Random House LLC. rhcbooks.com
Educators and librarians, for a variety of teaching tools, visit us at RHTeachersLibrarians.com
Library of Congress Control Number: 2023951553
ISBN 978-0-593-71165-1 (trade) — ISBN 978-0-593-71166-8 (ebook)
Printed in the United States of America
10 9 8 7 6 5 4 3 2 1

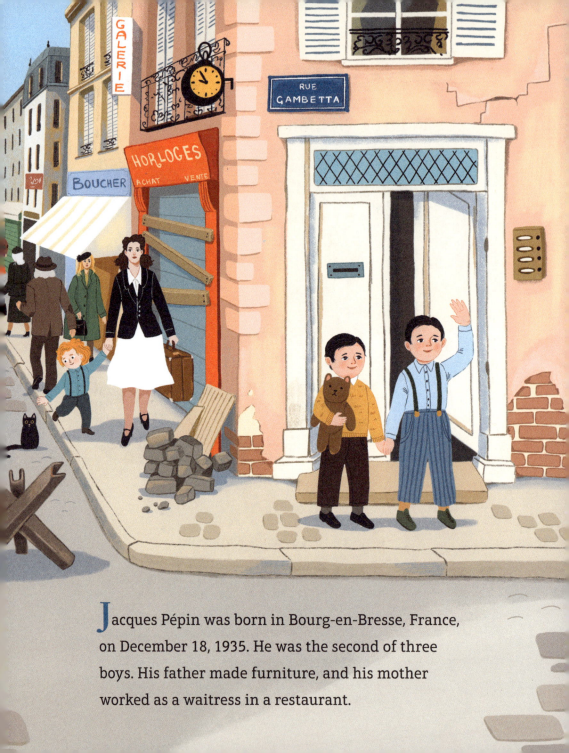

J acques Pépin was born in Bourg-en-Bresse, France, on December 18, 1935. He was the second of three boys. His father made furniture, and his mother worked as a waitress in a restaurant.

When Jacques was five years old, Germany invaded France—and World War II began. This led to big changes in his life.

Stores had limited food supplies. Jacques's mother had to ride her bicycle to farms outside of town to buy butter for their bread. His father joined a group of freedom fighters. It was dangerous, and he was rarely home.

Sometimes, planes flew low at night. Jacques's mother rushed the boys out of the apartment and hid beneath a nearby train underpass until they were gone.

One day, Jacques rode in a wagon towed behind his mother's bicycle. Miles later, they stopped at a farm. Chickens, ducks, geese, and some muddy pigs greeted him. Jacques's mother knew the farmer and his wife. Jacques would stay with them that summer. The country was safer than the town.

Jacques herded twelve cows out to the fields every day. He watched over them until it was time to bring them back to the barn in the evening. It was a big job for a six-year-old boy!

The farmer's wife showed Jacques how to milk a cow, and he drank his first bowl of warm, fresh milk. It tasted wonderful!

During the war, Jacques lived at home when school was in session and stayed on a farm each summer.

One day, he heard welcome news. France was free again! The war was over! People celebrated in the streets as an American tank rolled through town. Soldiers tossed treats to the children. Jacques enjoyed his very first chocolate bar.

Soon Jacques's father came home. The family was together again, and life was sweet.

Jacques's mother opened a restaurant, and all the Pépins helped out. After school, Jacques plunked his schoolbooks down, tied on an apron, and began peeling potatoes. He loved working in the kitchen—the smell of bread baking, the shine of the knives, and the sound of pans clattering filled him with joy.

After a long day of serving customers, his family ate dinner with the waitresses. Jacques was happier than ever. He decided to become a chef.

Jacques left school when he was thirteen years old to train as a chef at a hotel restaurant. Proudly, he donned his uniform. He lit the enormous stove, scrubbed pots, and chopped onions. There were no books to study or recipes to read. Jacques learned to cook by watching the chef.

After three years as an apprentice, Jacques understood food not just by taste and smell but by sight and sound, too. Scrambled eggs looked soft and velvety. Meat sizzled. Fresh beans snapped. He was a real chef!

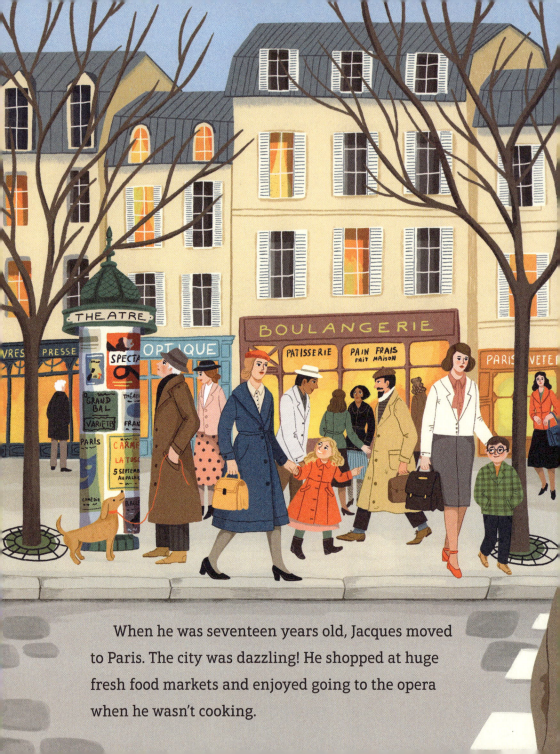

When he was seventeen years old, Jacques moved to Paris. The city was dazzling! He shopped at huge fresh food markets and enjoyed going to the opera when he wasn't cooking.

Jacques worked in some of Paris's best restaurants. For a time, he was even the personal chef for three prime ministers of France!

Jacques got a job at a French restaurant but fell in love with American street food—pizza, hot dogs, and popcorn. He made friends easily, including the famous chef Julia Child. They often cooked for each other.

Once, he was invited to a friend's house for dinner. Everyone began eating roast beef and mashed potatoes. Jacques sat there and waited for the bread. Then he realized that bread and butter might be present on a table in France, but not in New York!

America was an amazing place. Though he had quit school as a teenager, he went to college in New York to learn English. He loved school so much he earned two degrees.

Jacques was asked to be the White House chef for President Kennedy, *and* he was offered a job at Howard Johnson's, a chain of restaurants across the country. Jacques didn't want to move to Washington, DC, so he decided to create new recipes for the popular restaurant.

Jacques was already a top chef, but he began as a line cook at a Howard Johnson's. He knew he had to learn this new job as a beginner.

In 1966, Jacques married Gloria Augier. Their daughter, Claudine, was born a year and a half later.

Jacques and Gloria fixed up an old house in the Catskill Mountains. They planted a vegetable garden. Jacques opened his own restaurant in the city and drove home to the country at the end of each day. Life was great . . . until the night a deer jumped in front of his car.

Jacques suffered many injuries in the crash. When he recovered, he could no longer stand all day in a kitchen.

But he could teach! He taught cooking in classrooms and on television. He asked the camera person to focus on his hands so viewers could see *how* to make a dish. He even showed audiences how to carve a lemon to look like a pig! He also wrote many cookbooks to share his knowledge with even more home cooks.

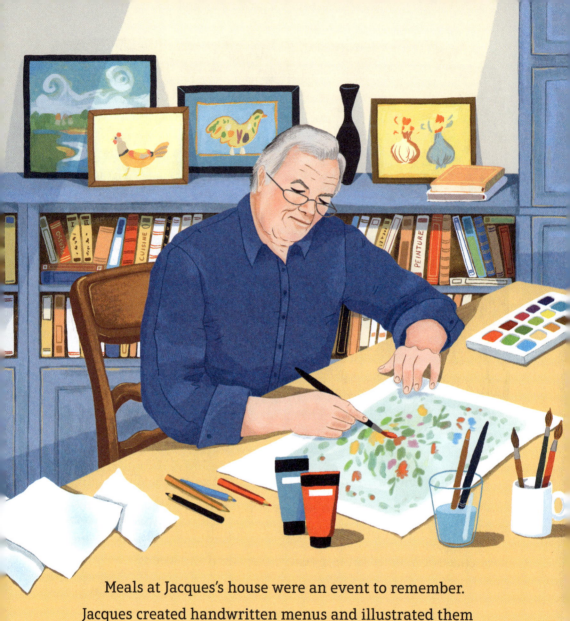

Meals at Jacques's house were an event to remember. Jacques created handwritten menus and illustrated them with little drawings. Drawing led to painting. His favorite subject to paint is chickens. He's made more than one hundred chicken paintings!

Jacques traveled from coast to coast, trying different kinds of food. He sampled Chinese, Indian, Italian, Japanese, Mexican, and Southern cuisine. He cooked these new dishes. Soon he felt he was no longer a French chef but an *American* chef.

He created the Jacques Pépin Foundation, giving people who need a fresh start the chance to learn food service skills. He had been given a new start in America when he first arrived and wanted others to have the same opportunity.

For more than seventy years, Jacques Pépin has cooked and enjoyed the finest meals. Yet his favorite food is good bread with fresh butter. A simple meal, he believes, tastes better when shared with friends.